Road Trip: Famous Routes

# The PACIFIC COAST HIGHWAY

## BY BENJAMIN PROUDFIT

Gareth Stevens
PUBLISHING

Please visit our website, www.garethstevens.com. For a free color catalog of all our high-quality books, call toll free 1-800-542-2595 or fax 1-877-542-2596.

**Library of Congress Cataloging-in-Publication Data**

Names: Proudfit, Benjamin, author.
Title: The Pacific Coast Highway / Benjamin Proudfit.
Description: New York : Gareth Stevens Pub., [2017] | Series: Road trip:
  famous routes | Includes index.
Identifiers: LCCN 2016008673 | ISBN 9781482446685 (pbk.) | ISBN 9781482446678 (library bound) | ISBN 9781482449464 (6 pack)
Subjects: LCSH: Pacific Coast Highway–Juvenile literature. | Automobile
  travel–California–Pacific Coast–Juvenile literature.
Classification: LCC F859.3 .P67 2017 | DDC 979.4–dc23
LC record available at http://lccn.loc.gov/2016008673

First Edition

Published in 2017 by
**Gareth Stevens Publishing**
111 East 14th Street, Suite 349
New York, NY 10003

Designer: Andrea Davison-Bartolotta
Editor: Kristen Nelson

Photo credits: Cover, p. 1 (top) Andrew Zarivny/Shutterstock.com; cover, p. 1 (bottom) Pung/Shutterstock.com; p. 4 LagunaticPhoto/Shutterstock.com; p. 5 Doug Meek/Shutterstock.com; p. 6 Kim Steele/Stockbyte/Getty Images; p. 7 Michael Warwick/Shutterstock.com; p. 8 Everett Historical/Shutterstock.com; p. 9 B. Anthony Stewart/National Geographic/Getty Images; p. 10 Allen J. Schaben/Los Angeles Times/Getty Images; p. 11 Brian van der Brug/ Los Angeles Times/Getty Images; p. 12 Stephen Dunn/Getty Images; p. 13 agaliza/iStock/Thinkstock; p. 14 Richard Fitzer/Shutterstock.com; p. 15 Sydneymills/Shutterstock.com; p. 16 SvetlanaSF/Shutterstock.com; p. 17 (main) Ricardo DeAratanha/Los Angeles Times/Getty Images; p. 17 (inset) Panoramic Images/Getty Images; p. 18 f11photo/ Shutterstock.com; p. 19 Mark Ralston/AFP/Getty Images; p. 20 (top) Mariusz S. Jurgielewicz/Shutterstock.com; p. 20 (bottom) Frederic J. Brown/AFP/Getty Images; p. 21 courtesy of the Library of Congress.

Printed in the United States of America

CPSIA compliance information: Batch #CS16GS: For further information contact Gareth Stevens, New York, New York at 1-800-542-2595.

# Contents

Words in the glossary appear in **bold** type the first time they are used in the text.

# The PCH

Surf's up! In order to take one of the best road trips in the United States, you'll need to head to the West Coast. The Pacific Coast Highway—or PCH as it's often called—runs *right* on the edge of California.

The official PCH is fewer than 130 miles (209 km) long, **stretching** between Dana Point, California, and Oxnard, California. However, it's part of California **Route** 1, which is sometimes also called the Pacific Coast Highway. It runs along the Pacific Coast for about 655 miles (1,054 km).

## Pit Stop

California Route 1 is commonly just called "the One" by locals.

# All About the
# Pacific Coast Highway

**where found:** California

**year established:** opened as part of the Roosevelt Highway in 1929; renamed the Pacific Coast Highway in 1941

**length:** officially less than 130 miles (209 km)

**number of drivers yearly:** millions of both **tourists** and Californians

**major attractions:** Los Angeles, California; California missions; Año Nuevo Natural Preserve; many beaches; Santa Monica Mountains National Recreation Area

When talking about the PCH, many people mean all the coastal highways between San Francisco, California, and San Diego, California. This book will cover fun stops on both the official PCH and beyond!

# The Idea Forms

In 1894, Dr. John Roberts was called to help people in a shipwreck at Point Sur. It took him almost 4 hours to reach them from his Monterey Peninsula home. This **convinced** him an official road would help travelers and increase business opportunities along the coast. He began telling others about the idea!

Plans for a highway on the California coast began in 1919. During its construction, workers had to use an explosive called dynamite to shape the rocky cliffs overlooking the Pacific Ocean.

A number of bridges were needed when building the coastal highway. The most famous of these might be Bixby Bridge north of Big Sur, California, on the One.

# Roosevelt Highway

The entire highway was completed in the 1930s. It was joined to roadways to the north and south to make it connect the Canadian and Mexican borders. Altogether, the highway was called Roosevelt Highway, but different parts of it have been renamed since. The part that's called the Pacific Coast Highway today was named in 1941.

When first built, Roosevelt Highway was Route 60. It's also been Route 3 and Route 101 **Alternate**. Signs calling it Route 1 went up in 1964.

**Theodore Roosevelt**

## Pit Stop

Roosevelt Highway was named for President Theodore Roosevelt.

In order to build the Pacific Coast Highway on California's rocky coast, some supplies and tools had to be brought in by boat!

9

# Beauty on the Highway

If you love scenic views of the ocean, spending time driving the PCH is worth it! There are some steep drops and somewhat dangerous curves on the road that many people find exciting.

Along the road are many turnoffs for those traveling by car to stop and check out the crashing waves of the Pacific. Or you can easily stop and enjoy the sun at one of the many beaches on the California coast.

whale-watching tour

DANA PRIDE

## Pit Stop

At the southern end of the official PCH, Dana Point is a great place to try whale watching! The city even has a Festival of Whales every year.

**Landslides** can cause parts of the PCH to need repair. Storms, including those that cause big waves, also cause erosion, or wear, on the road.

# City of Angels

The PCH passes right through one of the most populated cities in the world: Los Angeles. No road trip along the PCH would be complete without a few days in the "City of Angels."

You can see famous works of art *and* play at the Los Angeles County Museum of Modern Art. Family Sundays include cool talks and activities for everyone on your road trip! Los Angeles also has a huge zoo with special rainforest and elephant **habitats**.

**Santa Monica Pier**

## Pit Stop

Some of California's most famous beach areas aren't far from LA. Long Beach, Newport Beach, and Santa Monica all have fun waterfronts that are great for sunbathing, people watching, and more.

Los Angeles is home to more than 10.1 million people—and that's not counting the millions of tourists who visit!

# Hit the Trails

A road trip along the California coast can include many amazing natural sights!

The Santa Monica Mountains are right outside of LA. The national recreation area around them has more than 500 miles (805 km) of hiking trails for runners, bikers, and even those on horseback. In fact, visitors can rent a horse and take a guided tour of the beautiful mountain views. While exploring the area, you might see a coyote, dolphin, quail, or even a mountain lion!

## Pit Stop

Seal Beach National Wildlife **Refuge** is home to many **endangered** animals, including peregrine falcons, round stingrays, and green sea turtles. Visitors can only tour this wetland once a month, so check the refuge's website before you go.

Because of the location of the Santa Monica Mountains National Recreation Area, visitors can enjoy pleasant weather year round for their outdoor activities.

# North on the One

A road trip on the PCH is a great jumping-off point to see even more of the California coast. Driving north on California Route 1 from the official PCH takes you to Santa Barbara, which has beautiful sandy beaches right on the Pacific Ocean.

Another beach town north on the One is San Simeon, home to Hearst Castle! Visitors can tour the castle, which sits on 127 acres (51 ha). It has 115 rooms and displays the art collection of wealthy newspaperman William Randolph Hearst.

## Pit Stop

When taking California Route 1, San Francisco is about 415 miles (668 km) north of the PCH. There, you can see—and even walk across—the Golden Gate Bridge!

About 250 miles (400 km) north of Oxnard (the north end of the PCH) is Big Sur, a popular vacation spot. In Pfeiffer Big Sur State Park, visitors can stay in forests of huge redwood trees and see lots of wildlife.

Hearst Castle

# South to San Diego

Dana Point marks the southern end of both the PCH and California Route 1. But there's a lot to see if you continue your road trip in Southern California.

Those traveling to San Diego shouldn't miss the famous San Diego Zoo! It's home to more than 3,500 endangered or **rare** animals that live in natural-looking habitats. There's also the San Diego Zoo Safari Park, where visitors can ride a **tram** through an African habitat to see many animals, including giraffes and rhinos.

## Pit Stop

Want to pretend to be a pirate? Climb aboard steamboats, submarines, and sailing ships at the Maritime Museum of San Diego!

18

Many visitors have a chance to meet animals at the San Diego Zoo!

# California History

Along the coast of California, Spanish settlers built 21 missions in the late 1700s. Missions were places where Spanish settlers and priests lived and tried to **convert** native peoples to Christianity. These are great places to learn about the history of California's founding.

The missions of San Fernando Rey de España and San Gabriel Archángel are found close to the PCH. They both show off the pretty Spanish **architecture** that **influenced** the look of many other places in California.

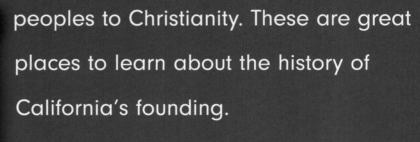

San Fernando Rey de España

San Gabriel Archángel

# California Missions

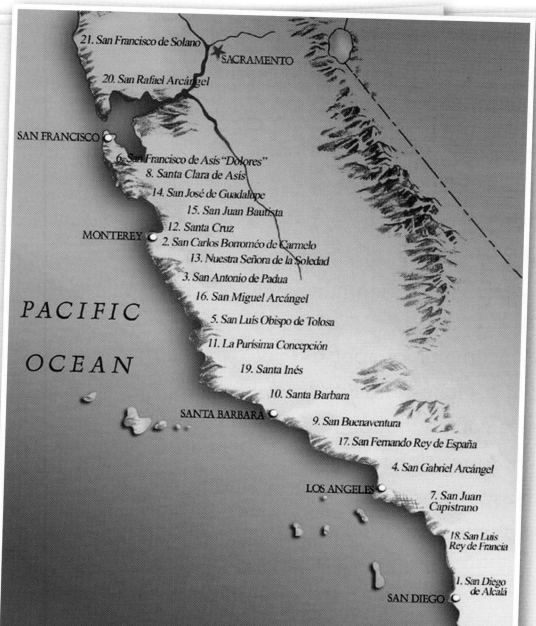

21. San Francisco de Solano

★ SACRAMENTO

20. San Rafael Arcángel

SAN FRANCISCO ○

6. San Francisco de Asís "Dolores"
8. Santa Clara de Asís
14. San José de Guadalupe
15. San Juan Bautista
12. Santa Cruz
MONTEREY ○ 2. San Carlos Borroméo de Carmelo
13. Nuestra Señora de la Soledad
3. San Antonio de Padua
16. San Miguel Arcángel
5. San Luis Obispo de Tolosa
11. La Purísima Concepción
19. Santa Inés
10. Santa Barbara
SANTA BARBARA ○
9. San Buenaventura
17. San Fernando Rey de España
4. San Gabriel Arcángel
LOS ANGELES ○
7. San Juan Capistrano
18. San Luis Rey de Francia
1. San Diego de Alcalá
SAN DIEGO ○

PACIFIC OCEAN

# Glossary

**alternate:** one of two or more choices

**architecture:** the construction and style of a building

**convert:** to try to change someone's faith

**convince:** to cause to have belief

**endangered:** in danger of dying out

**habitat:** the natural place where an animal or plant lives

**influence:** to have an effect on

**landslide:** the sudden movement of rocks and dirt down a hill or mountain

**rare:** uncommon or special

**refuge:** a place set aside for wild animals to live safely

**route:** a course that people travel

**stretch:** to reach across

**tourist:** someone who comes to visit a place

**tram:** a type of train that has cars with open windows and goes slower than regular trains

# For More Information

## Books

Bartley, Niccole. *The West Coast.* New York, NY: PowerKids Press, 2015.

Gregersen, Erik. *The Complete History of Wheeled Transportation: From Cars and Trucks to Buses and Bikes.* New York, NY: Britannica Educational Publishing, 2012.

Kirchner, Jason. *California.* North Mankato, MN: Next Page, 2017.

## Websites

**Pacific Coast Highway–South**
*visitcalifornia.com/trip/pacific-coast-highway-south*
See pictures and read more about places to stop along the PCH.

**The U.S. Highway System**
*factmonster.com/ipka/A0881994.html*
Find out about the history of highways in the United States.

# Index